SIMPLY SOLIDS™

A Twist on the Traditional Use of Solid Fabrics

Edited by Carolyn S. Vagts

Annie's™

Introduction

The designers for *Simply Solids* have blended quilts from the past and present into a collection of must-have patterns. Take a walk on the creative side through these pages and see what's in store. As always, our designers have taken the challenge set before them, and again, they have surpassed our expectations.

Simply Solids is full of exceptional ideas for the use of solid fabrics and designs with a twist on tradition. Solids are not just for the modern quilter. Solid fabrics work wonderfully in all styles of quilts from primitive to contemporary.

This book is a collection of patterns that speak to all quilters. We have something for everyone at all skill levels, beginner to advanced. It's time to revisit a classic fabric with an open mind.

Happy quilting!

Carolyn L. Vagts

Table of Contents

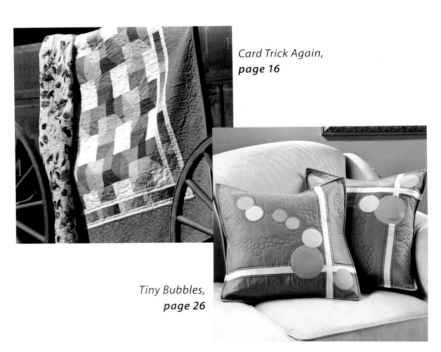

Card Trick Again,
page 16

Tiny Bubbles,
page 26

Spools & Buttons

Design by Avis Shirer

Create a modern country feel with solid fabrics, a traditional block pattern and a bit of appliqué. It's easier than it looks.

Project Specifications

Skill Level: Confident Beginner
Quilt Size: 53" x 62"
Block Size: 9" x 9"
Number of Blocks: 30

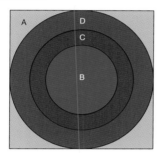

Button
9" x 9" Block
Make 15

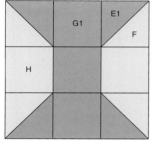

Gray Spool
9" x 9" Block
Make 7

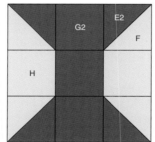

Black Spool
9" x 9" Block
Make 8

Materials

- ⅜ yard each 14 assorted solids
- ⅞ yard dark gray solid
- ⅞ yard tan solid
- 1½ yards black solid
- 1⅝ yards light brown solid
- Backing 62" x 70"
- Batting 62" x 70"
- All-purpose thread to match fabrics
- Quilting thread
- 2½ yards red dot tracing material
- Basic sewing tools and supplies

Cutting

1. Trace 15 each of circle patterns (B, C and D) given onto red dot tracing material. Cut out the circles, leaving a ¼" margin around each one.

2. Cut two 3⅞" by fabric width strips dark gray solid; subcut strips into 14 (3⅞") E1 squares.

3. Cut two 3½" by fabric width strips dark gray solid; subcut strips into 21 (3½") G1 squares.

4. Cut three 3½" by fabric width strips dark gray solid; subcut strips into two 3½" x 16" L strips and two 3½" x 19" K strips. Cut a total of four 3½" M squares from the remainder of these strips.

5. Cut three 3⅞" by fabric width strips tan solid; subcut strips into 30 (3⅞") F squares.

6. Cut three 3½" by fabric width strips tan solid; subcut strips into 30 (3½") H squares.

7. Cut two 3⅞" by fabric width strips black solid; subcut strips into 16 (3⅞") E2 squares.

8. Cut two 3½" by fabric width strips black solid; subcut strips into 24 (3½") G2 squares.

9. Cut four 3½" by fabric width strips black solid; subcut strips into four 3½" x 16¼" N strips and four 3½" x 19¼" O strips.

10. Cut six 2¼" by fabric width strips black solid for binding.

11. Cut four 9½" by fabric width strips light brown solid; subcut strips into 15 (9½") A squares.

12. Cut six 1½" by fabric width I/J strips light brown solid.

Tip

There are several methods that will result in smooth, perfectly round circles.

Freezer-Paper Method

Cut freezer-paper circles using the inside stitching line on the patterns as the cutting line. Press the freezer-paper circles onto the wrong side of the fabric and cut the fabric ⅛"–¼" larger than the freezer-paper circles all around. Use the tip of an iron to press the fabric edges over the freezer-paper edges.

Cardboard Method

Use a sturdy but flexible cardboard to make a template the size of the finished circle. Cut a fabric circle using the pattern given. Stitch a basting line on the seam line all around the fabric circle. Place the fabric circle right side up on the cardboard circle and pull one of the basting threads to gather the circle around the cardboard and press to hold. Remove the cardboard circle.

Stabilizer Method

Use lightweight interfacing or a product such as the red dot tracing material recommended for the Spools & Buttons pattern. In this method, sewing the fabric circle to the interfacing or other stabilizer, results in a smooth circle when the fabric circle is turned right side out and pressed.

Completing the Button Blocks

1. Place the traced red dot tracing material circles on the right side of the assorted solids and stitch around each one on the marked line. Cut out each circle ⅛"–¼" beyond the stitched line.

2. Cut a slit in the red dot tracing material side of the stitched units and turn right side out. Press edges in a smooth curve, pressing the red dot tracing material to the wrong side.

3. After pressing, trim the red dot tracing material close to edges to reduce bulk.

4. Select and center a B circle on a C circle and appliqué in place using your favorite method. Center the stitched B-C circle on a D circle and appliqué in place to complete one circle unit as shown in Figure 1. Repeat to make a total of 15 circle units.

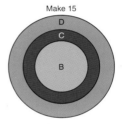

Make 15

Figure 1

5. Center and appliqué a circle unit on an A square to complete one Button block referring to the block drawing. Repeat to complete a total of 15 Button blocks.

Completing the Spool Blocks

1. Mark a diagonal line from corner to corner on the wrong side of each F square.

2. Place a marked F square right sides together with a E1 square and stitch ¼" on both sides of the marked line as shown in Figure 2. Cut apart on the marked line and press open with seam toward E1 to complete two E1-F units, again referring to Figure 2.

Figure 2

3. Repeat step 2 with remaining F squares, E1 squares and E2 squares to make a total of 28 E1-F and 32 E2-F units.

4. To complete one Gray Spool block, select four E1-F units, two H squares and three G1 squares.

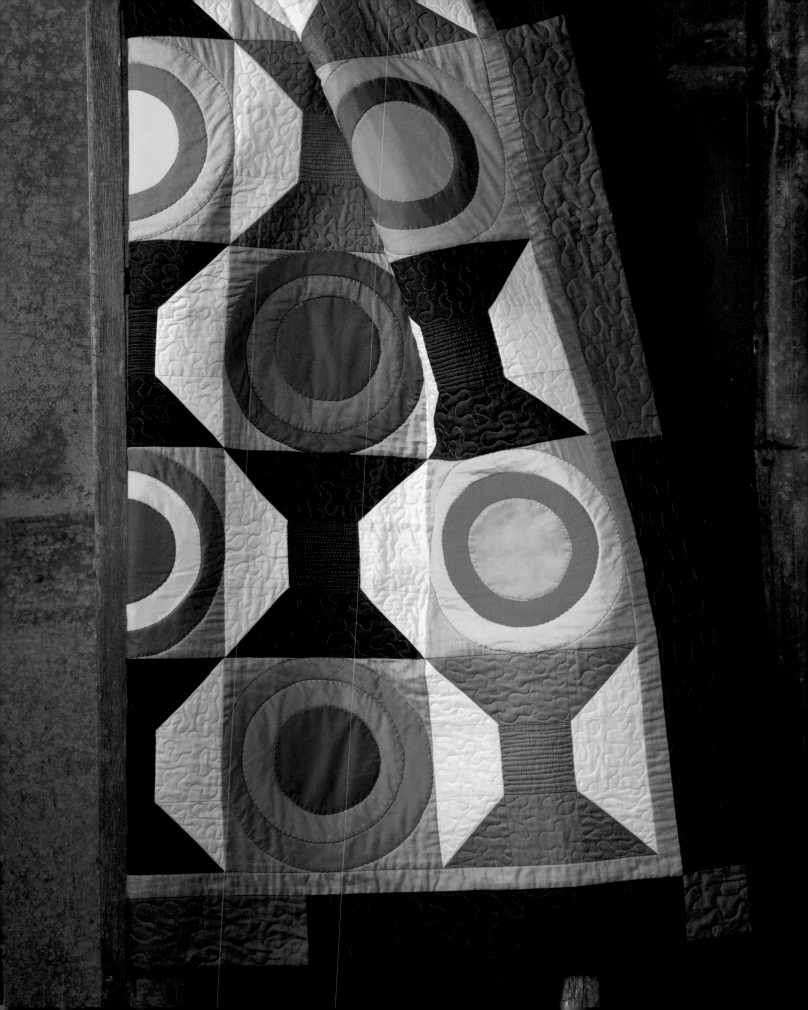

5. Join the three G1 squares to make the vertical center row; press seams away from the center square.

6. Sew an E1-F unit to opposite sides of an H square to make a side row as shown in Figure 3; press seams toward the H square. Repeat to make a second side row.

Make 2

Figure 3

7. Join the rows to complete one Gray Spool block referring to Figure 4; press seams in one direction.

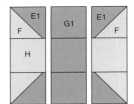

Figure 4

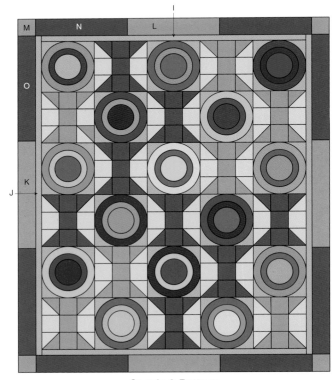

Spools & Buttons
Placement Diagram 53" x 62"

8. Repeat steps 4–7 to complete a total of seven Gray Spool blocks.

9. Repeat steps 4–7 with E2-F units and G2 and H squares to complete a total of eight Black Spool blocks referring to Figure 5.

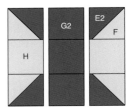

Figure 5

Completing the Quilt Top

1. Select and join one each Black Spool and Gray Spool block and three Button blocks to make an X row referring to Figure 6; press seams toward Button blocks. Repeat to make a total of three X rows.

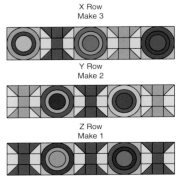

X Row
Make 3

Y Row
Make 2

Z Row
Make 1

Figure 6

2. Join one Black Spool block with two each Button and Gray Spool blocks to complete a Y row, again referring to Figure 6; press seams toward the Button blocks. Repeat to make a total of two Y rows.

3. Join three Black Spool blocks with two Button blocks to make a Z row, again referring to Figure 6; press seams in one direction.

4. Join the X, Y and Z rows to complete the pieced center; press seams in one direction.

5. Join the I/J strips on the short ends to make a long strip; press seams open. Subcut strip into two 1½" x 45½" I strips and two 1½" x 56½" J strips.

6. Sew the I strips to the top and bottom and J strips to opposite long sides of the pieced center; press seams toward the I and J strips.

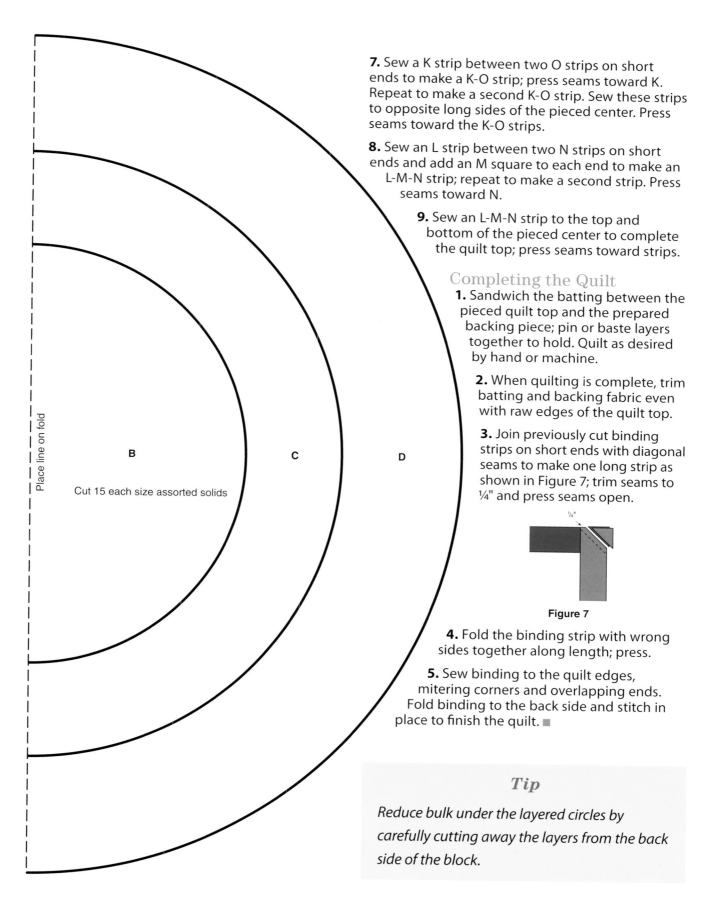

Place line on fold

B

Cut 15 each size assorted solids

C

D

7. Sew a K strip between two O strips on short ends to make a K-O strip; press seams toward K. Repeat to make a second K-O strip. Sew these strips to opposite long sides of the pieced center. Press seams toward the K-O strips.

8. Sew an L strip between two N strips on short ends and add an M square to each end to make an L-M-N strip; repeat to make a second strip. Press seams toward N.

9. Sew an L-M-N strip to the top and bottom of the pieced center to complete the quilt top; press seams toward strips.

Completing the Quilt

1. Sandwich the batting between the pieced quilt top and the prepared backing piece; pin or baste layers together to hold. Quilt as desired by hand or machine.

2. When quilting is complete, trim batting and backing fabric even with raw edges of the quilt top.

3. Join previously cut binding strips on short ends with diagonal seams to make one long strip as shown in Figure 7; trim seams to ¼" and press seams open.

¼"

Figure 7

4. Fold the binding strip with wrong sides together along length; press.

5. Sew binding to the quilt edges, mitering corners and overlapping ends. Fold binding to the back side and stitch in place to finish the quilt. ■

Tip

Reduce bulk under the layered circles by carefully cutting away the layers from the back side of the block.

Bricks & Bubbles

Design by Chris Malone

This design is so versatile. You can use the finished runner as a wall hanging or on a table. Change the colors to coordinate with your decor.

Project Specifications
Skill Level: Confident Beginner
Runner Size: 12" x 60"

Materials
- 15 (2½" x 42") strips in 5 ivory/tan solids
- ½ yard aqua solid
- Backing 20" x 68"
- Batting 20" x 68"
- All-purpose thread to match fabrics
- Quilting thread
- Compass (optional)
- Freezer paper
- Basic sewing tools and supplies

Cutting
1. Set aside four of the 2½" x 42" ivory/tan strips for binding.

2. From the remaining 11 (2½" x 42") ivory/tan strips, cut the following: 10 (2½" x 3½") A, 19 (2½" x 4½") B, 17 (2½" x 5½") C, eight 2½" x 6½" D, nine 2½" x 7½" E, five 2½" x 8½" F and two 2½" x 9½" G. *Note: Use a variety of ivory/tan strips when cutting each lettered piece.*

3. Use circle patterns given or a compass (or cups, bowls, etc.) to draw circle patterns in each of the following sizes onto the matte side of freezer paper: 3", 4½", 5½" and 6½".

4. Cut out and iron freezer-paper circles, shiny side down, onto the wrong side of the aqua solid leaving ½" between circles; cut around circles leaving a ³/₁₆" seam allowance.

Tip
Before pressing fabric over freezer paper, dab a little spray starch on the folded-over edge of the circles with a cotton-tip swab and re-press for a firmer hold.

5. Using the side of your iron, fold the fabric over the edge of the paper circle and press; clip seam as needed to help fabric lie flat, as shown in Figure 1. Continue all around the circle until the seam allowance is pressed inside. Remove freezer-paper circle.

Figure 1

6. Repeat step 5 with remaining circles to make six (3") and three each 4½", 5½" and 6½" fabric circles. *Note: The freezer paper patterns may be reused.*

Completing the Runner Top
1. Arrange and join the A, B, C, D, E, F and G pieces in 30 rows of two or thee strips each referring to Figure 2; press seams open. Join the rows to complete the pieced background; press seams open.

2. Using the Placement Diagram and project photo for guides, arrange the aqua circles on the long pieced background. *Note: The top and bottom both have a circle that hangs off the edge.*

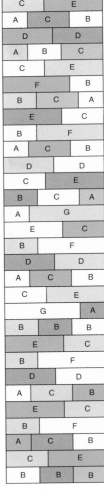

Figure 2

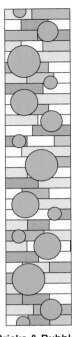

Bricks & Bubbles
Placement Diagram 12" x 60"

3. When pleased with the arrangement, pin or baste the circles in place and trim excess fabric on the two extended circles even with the background edges.

4. Appliqué circles in place using your favorite stitching method to complete the runner top.

Completing the Quilt

1. Sandwich the batting between the pieced quilt top and the prepared backing piece; pin or baste layers together to hold. Quilt as desired by hand or machine.

2. When quilting is complete, trim batting and backing fabric even with raw edges of the quilt top.

3. Join previously cut binding strips on short ends with diagonal seams to make one long strip as shown in Figure 3; trim seams to ¼" and press seams open.

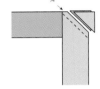

Figure 3

4. Fold the binding strip with wrong sides together along length; press.

5. Sew binding to the quilt edges, mitering corners and overlapping ends. Fold binding to the back side and stitch in place to finish the quilt. ■

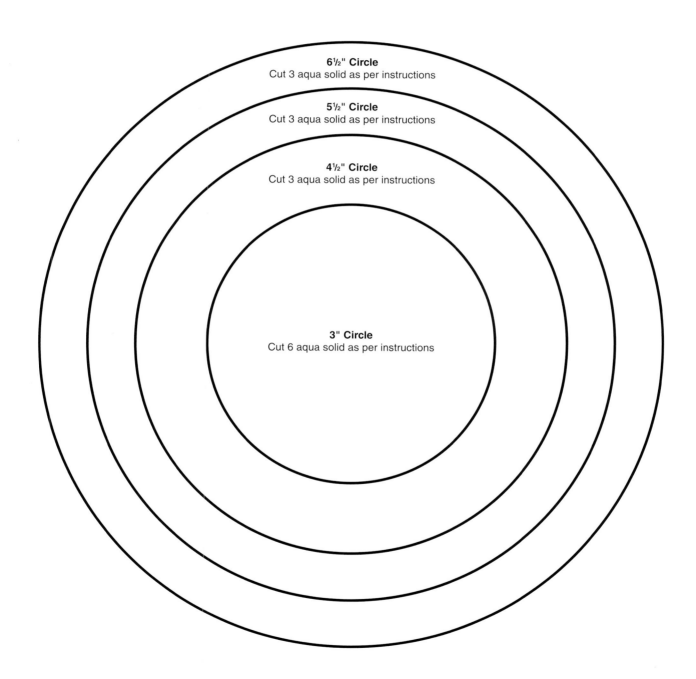

6½" Circle
Cut 3 aqua solid as per instructions

5½" Circle
Cut 3 aqua solid as per instructions

4½" Circle
Cut 3 aqua solid as per instructions

3" Circle
Cut 6 aqua solid as per instructions

Quick Step

Design by Gina Gempesaw
Quilted by Carole Whaling

A traditionally pieced block pattern, a white solid background and a touch of fusible appliqué is all you need to create this lovely quilt.

Project Specifications
Skill Level: Confident Beginner
Quilt Size: 73" x 91½"
Block Size: 16" x 16"
Number of Blocks: 12

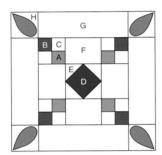

Teardrop
16" x 16" Block
Make 12

Materials
- ½ yard dark green solid
- ⅝ yard light purple solid
- ¾ yard light green solid
- 1⅛ yards dark purple solid
- 5¾ yards white solid
- Backing 81" x 100"
- Batting 81" x 100"
- All-purpose thread to match fabrics
- Quilting thread
- Invisible thread (optional)
- 1 yard 18"-wide fusible web
- Template material
- Basic sewing tools and supplies

Cutting
1. Cut three 2" by fabric width B strips dark green solid.

2. Cut two 3" by fabric width strips dark green solid; subcut strips into 20 (3") J squares.

3. Cut three 2" by fabric width A strips light green solid.

4. Cut seven 2" by fabric width K/L strips light green solid.

5. Cut one 3⅜" by fabric width strip dark purple solid; subcut strip into 12 (3⅜") D squares.

6. Cut nine 2¼" by fabric width strips dark purple solid for binding.

7. Cut six 2" by fabric width C strips white solid.

8. Cut two 2⅞" by fabric width strips white solid; subcut strips into 24 (2⅞") squares. Cut each square in half on one diagonal to make 48 E triangles.

9. Cut four 4½" by fabric width strips white solid; subcut strips into 48 (3½" x 4½") F rectangles.

10. Cut four 10½" by fabric width strips white solid; subcut strips into 48 (3½" x 10½") G strips.

11. Cut 16 (3" by fabric width) strips white solid; subcut strips into 31 (3" x 16½") I strips.

12. Cut two 6½" x 80" M strips and two 6½" x 73½" N strips along the length of the white solid.

13. Cut three 4" strips along the fabric length of the leftover width of white solid; subcut strips into 48 (4") H squares. *Note: The H squares will be trimmed after teardrop shapes have been appliquéd to them.*

Completing the Appliqué
1. Prepare a template for the teardrop pattern given on page 15. Trace the teardrop shape on the paper side of fusible web 48 times.

2. Fuse the traced teardrops to the wrong side of the light purple solid, cut out on traced lines and remove paper backing.

3. Center diagonally and fuse one teardrop onto an H square. Stitch the teardrop in place using your favorite appliqué method. *Note: The sample used invisible thread and a machine blanket stitch for appliqué.*

4. When all teardrops have been appliquéd, trim H to 3½" square, keeping the teardrop centered on the diagonal of the square.

Completing the Teardrop Blocks

1. Sew a B strip to a C strip along the length to make a B-C strip set; press seam toward B. Repeat to make a total of three B-C strip sets.

2. Subcut the B-C strip sets into 48 (2") B-C units as shown in Figure 1.

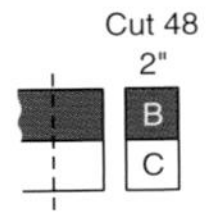

Cut 48
2"

Figure 1

3. Sew an A strip to a C strip along the length to make an A-C strip set; press seams toward A. Repeat to make a total of three A-C strip sets.

4. Subcut the A-C strip sets into 48 (2") A-C units as shown in Figure 2.

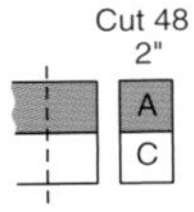

Cut 48
2"

Figure 2

5. Select and join one each A-C and B-C unit to complete a Four-Patch unit as shown in Figure 3; press seam to one side. Repeat to make a total of 48 Four-Patch units.

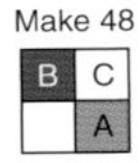

Make 48

Figure 3

6. Sew an E triangle to each side of a D square to make a D-E unit as shown in Figure 4; press seams toward E. Repeat to make a total of 12 D-E units. *Note: The D-E unit should measure 4½" square.*

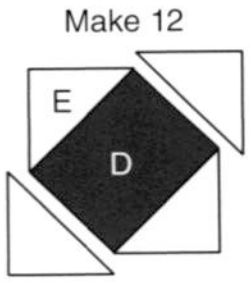

Make 12

Figure 4

7. To complete one Teardrop block, select one D-E unit, four Four-Patch units, four appliquéd H squares and four each F and G pieces.

8. Sew an F rectangle to opposite sides of the D-E unit to complete the center row as shown in Figure 5; press seams toward F.

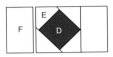

Figure 5

9. Sew a Four-Patch unit to opposite sides of an F rectangle to make the top row referring to Figure 6; press seams toward F. Repeat to make the bottom row.

Make 2

Figure 6

10. Sew the top and bottom rows to the center row to complete the block center referring to Figure 7; press seams away from the center row.

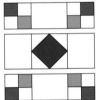

Figure 7

11. Sew a G strip to opposite sides of the block center referring to Figure 8; press seams toward G.

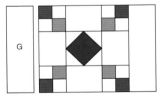

Figure 8

12. Sew an appliquéd H square to each end of two G strips referring to Figure 9; press seams toward G.

Figure 9

13. Sew the G-H units to opposite sides of the block center to complete one Teardrop block referring to Figure 10; press seams toward the G-H units.

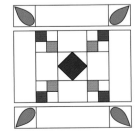

Figure 10

14. Repeat steps 7–13 to complete a total of 12 Teardrop blocks.

Completing the Quilt Top

1. Join three Teardrop blocks with four I strips to make a block row as shown in Figure 11; press seams toward I. Repeat to make a total of four block rows.

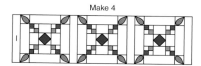

Make 4

Figure 11

2. Join three I strips with four J squares to make a sashing row referring to Figure 12; press seams toward I. Repeat to make a total of five sashing rows.

Make 5

Figure 12

3. Join the block rows with the sashing rows to complete the pieced center referring to the Placement Diagram for positioning; press seams toward sashing strips.

4. Join the K/L strips on the short ends to make a long strip; press seams open. Subcut strip into two 2" x 77" K strips and two 2" x 61½" L strips.

5. Sew K strips to opposite long sides and L strips to the top and bottom of the pieced center; press seams toward K and L strips.

6. Sew M strips to opposite long sides and N strips to the top and bottom of the pieced center to complete the quilt top; press seams toward the M and N strips.

Completing the Quilt

1. Sandwich the batting between the pieced quilt top and the prepared backing piece; pin or baste layers together to hold. Quilt as desired by hand or machine.

2. When quilting is complete, trim batting and backing fabric even with raw edges of the quilt top.

3. Join previously cut binding strips on short ends with diagonal seams to make one long strip as shown in Figure 13; trim seams to ¼" and press seams open.

¼"

Figure 13

4. Fold the binding strip with wrong sides together along length; press.

5. Sew binding to the quilt edges, mitering corners and overlapping ends. Fold binding to the back side and stitch in place to finish the quilt. ∎

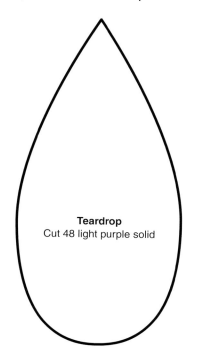

Teardrop
Cut 48 light purple solid

N

M K

Quick Step
Placement Diagram 73" x 91½"

Card Trick Again

Design by Sandra L. Hatch

This traditional block pattern is a Card Trick variation with a twist.

Project Specifications

Skill Level: Confident Beginner
Quilt Size: 72" x 96"
Block Size: 12" x 12"
Number of Blocks: 24

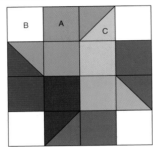

Card Trick Variation
12" x 12" Block
Make 24

Materials

- ⅞ yard each light aqua, light and dark pink, light and dark purple, and light and dark green solids*
- 1⅔ yards white solid
- 2⅞ yards dark aqua solid
- Backing 80" x 104"
- Batting 80" x 104"
- Neutral-color all-purpose thread
- Quilting thread
- Basic sewing tools and supplies

Cutting

1. Cut two 3½" by fabric width A strips from each of the ⅞-yard solid fabrics.

2. Cut two 3⅞" by fabric width strips from each of the ⅞-yard solid fabrics; subcut each color fabric into 12 (3⅞") C squares.

3. Cut two 2½" by fabric width F strips from each of the ⅞-yard solid fabrics.

4. Cut one 2¼" by fabric width strip from six of the ⅞-yard solid fabrics and two strips from one of the ⅞-yard solid fabrics. Cut strips in half to make two 2¼" x 21" binding strips from each strip.

5. Cut eight 3½" by fabric width B strips white solid; subcut four strips into 48 (3½") B squares. Set remaining four strips aside for strip sets.

6. Cut 13 (1½" by fabric width) D/E/G/H strips white solid.

7. Cut two 3½" by fabric width A strips dark aqua.

8. Cut two 3⅞" by fabric width strips dark aqua; subcut strips into 12 (3⅞") C squares.

9. Cut two 2½" by fabric width F strips dark aqua.

10. Cut one 2¼" by fabric width strip dark aqua. Cut strip in half to make two 2¼" x 21" binding strips.

11. Cut eight 8½" by fabric width I/J strips dark aqua.

Completing the Blocks

1. Mark a diagonal line on the wrong side of each light C square.

2. Select one marked light C square and pair up with a dark C square of the same color family with right sides together.

3. Referring to Figure 1, stitch ¼" on each side of the marked line. Cut apart on the marked line and press open to make two C units.

Figure 1

4. Repeat steps 2 and 3 to make a total of 24 C units in each of the four color variations as shown in Figure 2.

Make 24 each

Figure 2

5. Select one A strip each dark green, dark purple and light aqua; join along length in that order to make an A1 strip set. Repeat to make a second A1 strip set. Subcut the A1 strip sets into 24 (3½") A1 units as shown in Figure 3.

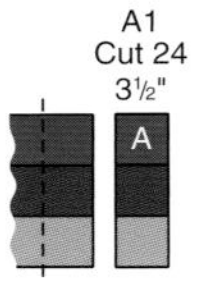

A1
Cut 24
3½"

Figure 3

6. Repeat step 5 with light green, light pink and dark aqua A strips to make two A2 strip sets; subcut the A2 strip sets into 24 (3½") A2 units referring to Figure 4.

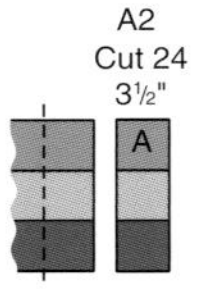

A2
Cut 24
3½"

Figure 4

7. Sew a B strip to a dark pink A strip to make an A-B1 strip set; repeat to make two strip sets. Subcut strip set into 24 (3½") A-B1 units as shown in Figure 5.

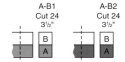

A-B1   A-B2
Cut 24   Cut 24
3½"   3½"

Figure 5

8. Repeat step 7 with remaining B strips and light purple A strips to make two A-B2 strip sets; subcut strip sets into 24 (3½") A-B2 units, again referring to Figure 5.

9. Select two B squares and one each A1, A2, A-B1 and A-B2 units and one of each C unit color variation. Arrange and join the units in rows and join the rows to complete one Card Trick Variation block referring to Figure 6.

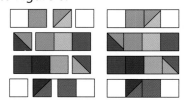

Figure 6

10. Repeat step 9 to make a total of 24 Card Trick Variation blocks.

Completing the Top

1. Arrange and join four Card Trick Variation blocks to make a row referring to Figure 7 for positioning of blocks; repeat to make six rows.

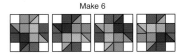

Make 6

Figure 7

2. Join the rows, turning every other row, to complete the pieced center referring to the Placement Diagram.

3. Join the D/E/G/H strips on the short ends to make a long strip; press seams open. Subcut strip into two strips in each of the following sizes: 1½" x 72½" D, 1½" x 50½" E, 1½" x 78½" G and 1½" x 56½" H.

4. Sew D strips to opposite long sides and E strips to the top and bottom of the pieced center.

5. Join one of each color F strip in any color order to make a strip set. Repeat to make two identical sets. Subcut strip sets into 17 (2½") F units as shown in Figure 8. *Note: You may be able to get 17 units from just one strip set.*

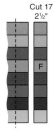

Cut 17
2½"

Figure 8

6. Join five F units and remove three squares from what will be the lower end to make the left side strip. Sew the removed squares to an F unit, continuing the color order; join this unit with two more F units to make the bottom strip. Repeat instructions for the left side strip to make the right side strip, removing the squares from what will be the upper end and adding the removed squares to the top strip, preserving the color order. Referring to the Placement Diagram, sew the side strips to the sides of the pieced center and then sew on the top and bottom strips.

7. Join the I/J strips on the short ends to make a long strip; press seams open. Subcut strip into two 8½" x 80½" I strips and two 8½" x 72½" J strips.

8. Sew G strips to opposite sides and H strips to the top and bottom of the pieced center. Repeat with the I and J strips to complete the pieced top.

Completing the Quilt

1. Sandwich the batting between the pieced quilt top and the prepared backing piece; pin or baste layers together to hold. Quilt as desired by hand or machine.

2. When quilting is complete, trim batting and backing fabric even with raw edges of the quilt top.

3. Keeping the same color order as the F units, join the previously cut binding strips on short ends with diagonal seams to make one long strip as shown in Figure 9; trim seams to ¼" and press seams open.

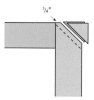

Figure 9

4. Fold the binding strip with wrong sides together along length; press.

5. Sew binding to the quilt edges, mitering corners and overlapping ends. Fold binding to the back side and stitch in place to finish the quilt. ■

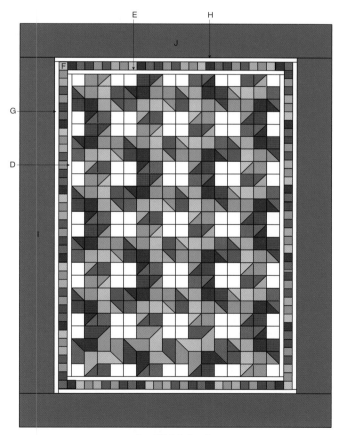

Card Trick Again
Placement Diagram 72" x 96"

Modern Country

Design by Wendy Sheppard

Update a primitive idea with vibrant solids
to create a modern country masterpiece.

Project Specifications
Skill Level: Intermediate
Runner Size: 22¼" x 50½"
Block Size: 9" x 9"
Number of Blocks: 3

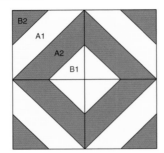

Modern Country
9" x 9" Block
Make 3

Materials
- 1 fat quarter black solid
- ¼ yard olive green solid
- 1⅛ yards light sage green solid
- 1¾ yards total assorted fall-palette solids (orange, gold, 2 yellows and green were used in the sample)
- 1½ yards cream solid
- Backing 31" x 59"
- Batting 31" x 59"
- Neutral-color all-purpose thread
- Quilting thread
- Brown embroidery floss
- 8" x 11" sheet fusible web (optional)
- 18 (⅜") burgundy buttons
- Basic sewing tools and supplies

Cutting
1. Make copies of paper-piecing patterns as directed on patterns.

2. Cut the assorted fall-palette solids into two or three fabric-width strips each 2" for D, 2½" for A2 and 3" for B2 for paper piecing.

3. Cut four each 2" C, 2½" A1 and 3" B1 fabric width strips cream solid for paper piecing. Cut more as needed when piecing.

4. Cut one 1⅞" by fabric width strip cream solid; subcut strip into four 1⅞" squares. Cut each 1⅞" square in half on one diagonal to make eight G triangles. Trim remainder of strip to 1½" and cut two 1½" F squares.

5. Cut four 1½" by fabric width strips olive green solid; subcut one strip into two 1½" x 16¾" I strips. Set aside remaining strips for H borders.

6. Cut three 1½" by fabric width strips light sage green solid; subcut strips into 12 (1½" x 9½") E strips.

7. Cut three 3½" by fabric width J strips light sage green solid.

8. Cut two 3½" x 22¾" K strips light sage green solid.

9. Cut four 2¼" by fabric width strips light sage green solid for binding.

10. Using pattern given, prepare bird shapes for your favorite method of appliqué using black solid.

Completing the Blocks
1. To make one block, use your favorite paper-piecing method and the A-B paper-piecing patterns to make four each A1-B2 and A2-B1 units, using the same fabric for pieces A2 and B2 within the same block referring to Figure 1.

Make 4 each

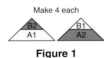

Figure 1

2. Join one each A1-B2 and A2-B1 unit to complete a block quarter as shown in Figure 2; press seams to one side. Repeat to make four block quarters. *Note: The paper can be removed from seam between the two pieces at this time, if you prefer.*

Make 4

Figure 2

3. Join the four block quarters to make one Modern Country block as shown in Figure 3; press.

Figure 3

4. Repeat steps 1–4 to complete a total of three different-color Modern Country blocks referring to the Placement Diagram for suggested colors.

Completing the Half Blocks

1. To complete one half block, prepare one each paper-pieced A1-B2 and A2-B1 units, and two C-D units (reversing the colors in one of the units to make a reversed C-D unit) using the same fabric for pieces A2, B2 and D within the same half block referring to Figure 4.

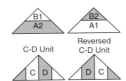

Figure 4

2. Join one each A1-B2 unit and A2-B1 unit to make a center unit as shown in Figure 5. Add a C-D and reversed C-D to adjacent sides of center unit, again referring to Figure 5 to complete one half block. *Note: Pay careful attention to the placement of color in each of the pieced units when making half blocks.*

Figure 5

3. Repeat steps 1 and 2 to complete a total of four different-color half blocks referring to the Placement Diagram for suggested colors.

Completing the Corner Units

1. Referring to the Placement Diagram for color suggestions, prepare eight paper-pieced C-D units, reversing the colors in four units to make reversed C-D units as shown in Figure 6.

Figure 6

2. Select one each same-fabric C-D and reversed C-D unit and join as shown in Figure 7 to complete one corner unit.

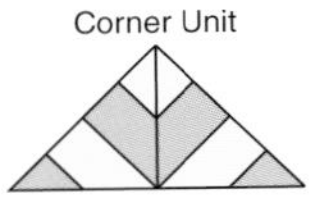

Corner Unit

Figure 7

3. Repeat step 2 to make a total of four different-color corner units.

Completing the Runner Top

1. Arrange and join the Modern Country blocks with the half blocks, corner units, E strips, F squares and G triangles in diagonal rows referring to Figure 8 for placement; press seams toward the E strips.

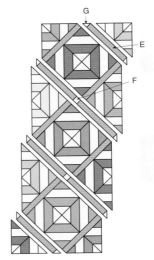

Figure 8

2. Join the rows to complete the pieced center; press seams toward E strips.

3. Join H strips on the short ends to make a long strip; press seams open. Subcut strip into two 1½" x 43" H strips.

4. Sew an H strip to opposite long sides and I strips to the short ends of the pieced center; press seams toward H and I strips.

5. Join J strips on the short ends to make a long strip; press seams open. Subcut strip into two 3½" x 45" J strips.

6. Sew J strips to opposite long sides and K strips to the short ends of the pieced center; press seams toward J and K strips.

7. Remove paper from all paper-pieced blocks, half blocks and corner units.

8. Apply one bird shape to opposite corners of the pieced top referring to the Placement Diagram for positioning.

9. Transfer the stem/button design to the pieced top.

10. Using 3 strands of brown embroidery floss, backstitch along the marked stem line.

Completing the Runner

1. Sandwich the batting between the pieced runner top and the prepared backing piece; pin or baste layers together to hold. Quilt as desired by hand or machine.

2. When quilting is complete, trim batting and backing fabric even with raw edges of the quilt top.

3. Join previously cut binding strips on short ends with diagonal seams to make one long strip as shown in Figure 9; trim seams to ¼" and press seams open.

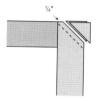

Figure 9

4. Fold the binding strip with wrong sides together along length; press.

5. Sew binding to the runner edges, mitering corners and overlapping ends. Fold binding to the back side and stitch in place.

6. Sew a button in place in marked locations to complete the quilt. ■

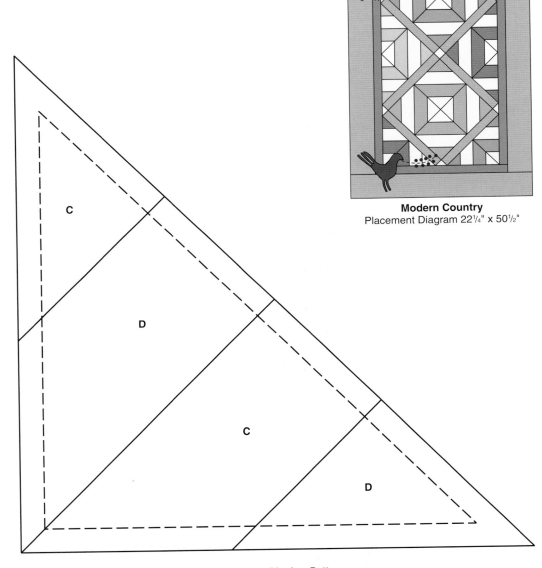

Modern Country
Placement Diagram 22¼" x 50½"

C-D Paper-Piecing Pattern
Make 16 copies
Each half block & each corner unit require 1 each C-D & C-D reversed units.

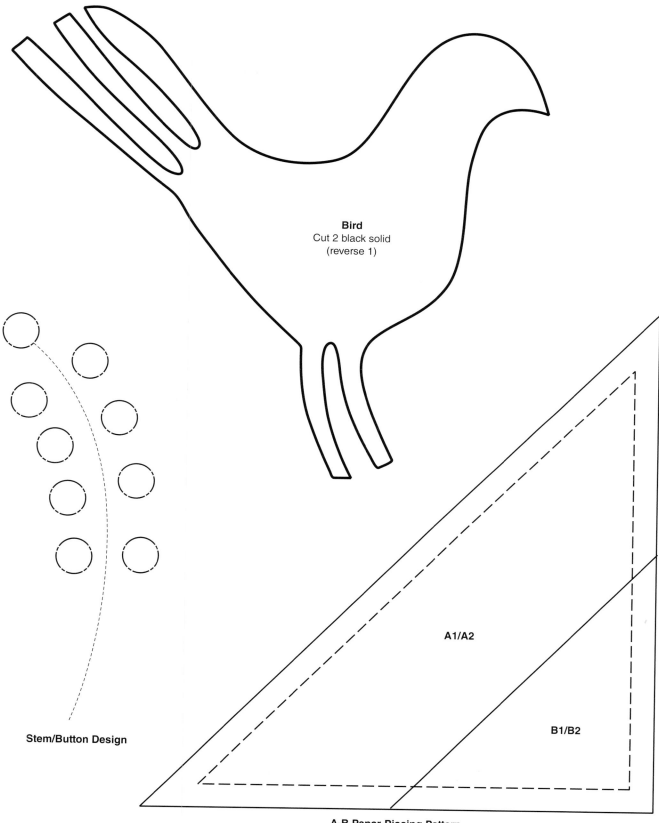

Bird
Cut 2 black solid
(reverse 1)

Stem/Button Design

A1/A2

B1/B2

A-B Paper-Piecing Pattern
Make 32 copies
Each full block requires 4 each A1-B2 & A2-B1 units.
Each half block requires 1 each A1-B2 & A2-B1.

Tiny Bubbles

Design by Carolyn S. Vagts for The Village Pattern Company

This pillow design makes a quick and easy project that can easily be adapted to any color theme. Make a set for yourself or to use as a gift.

Project Specifications
Skill Level: Beginner
Pillow Size: 20" x 20"

Materials
Materials listed will make 1 pillow.
- Scraps lime, aqua and yellow solids
- ⅛ yard cream solid
- ¾ yard muslin
- 1⅜ yards taupe solid
- Batting 24" x 24"
- All-purpose thread to match fabrics
- Quilting thread
- Template material
- ½ yard paper-release fusible web
- 20" x 20" pillow form
- Basic sewing tools and supplies

Cutting
1. Prepare templates for circle patterns given. Trace circles onto the paper side of the fusible web as directed on patterns for number to cut of each size and leaving ¼" between circles.

2. Cut out circles, leaving a ⅛" margin around each one. Fuse each fusible web circle to the wrong side of the lime, aqua or yellow solid scraps. Cut out circles on traced lines; remove paper backing.

3. Cut one 1½" by fabric width strip cream solid; subcut strip into one strip each of the following sizes: 1½" x 15½" E, 1½" x 20½" F and 1½" x 4½" G.

4. Cut one 24" by fabric width strip muslin; subcut strip into one 24" square for pillow top backing.

5. Cut one 26" by fabric width strip taupe solid; subcut strip into two 20½" x 26½" pillow back rectangles.

6. Cut one 15½" by fabric width strip taupe solid; subcut strip into one 15½" J square, two 4½" x 15½" H rectangles and one 4½" I square.

Completing the Pillow Top
1. Join the J square and one H rectangle with the E strip to make the J-E-H unit as shown in Figure 1; press seams toward E.

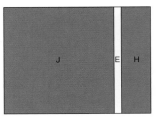

Figure 1

2. Join the remaining H rectangle and I square with the G strip to make the H-G-I unit as shown in Figure 2; press seams away from G.

Figure 2

3. Join the J-E-H unit and the H-G-I unit with the F strip to complete the pieced background as shown in Figure 3; press seams away from F.

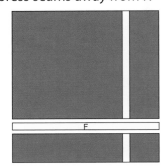

Figure 3

4. Arrange the prepared A, B, C and D circles on the pieced background and fuse in place referring to the Placement Diagram for positioning.

5. Stitch circle shapes in place using thread to match fabrics and your favorite machine-appliqué stitch to complete the pillow top.

28

Completing the Pillow

1. Place the muslin backing square on a flat surface; place the batting square on top of the muslin square. Center the pillow top right side up on top of the muslin/batting layer and pin layers together to hold.

2. Quilt as desired by hand or machine. When quilting is complete, trim muslin and batting layers even with the pillow top edges.

3. Fold each of the 20½" x 26" pillow back rectangles in half so they measure 20½" x 13" referring to Figure 4; press.

Figure 4

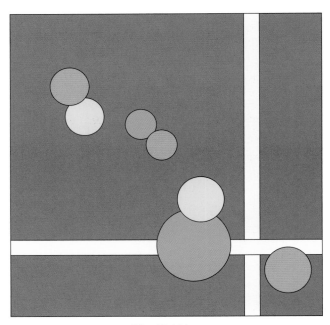

Tiny Bubbles
Placement Diagram 20" x 20"

4. Pin one of the pressed rectangles to the right side of the quilted pillow top matching raw edges as shown in Figure 5.

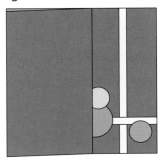

Figure 5

5. Pin the second pressed rectangle to the right side of the remaining end of the quilted pillow top, overlapping at the center referring to Figure 6.

Figure 6

6. Stitch all around outer edges of the pinned layers.

7. Trim corners and turn right side out through the opening at the overlapped edges and press flat.

8. Topstitch ¼" from outer edges all around.

9. Insert pillow form to finish. ■

28

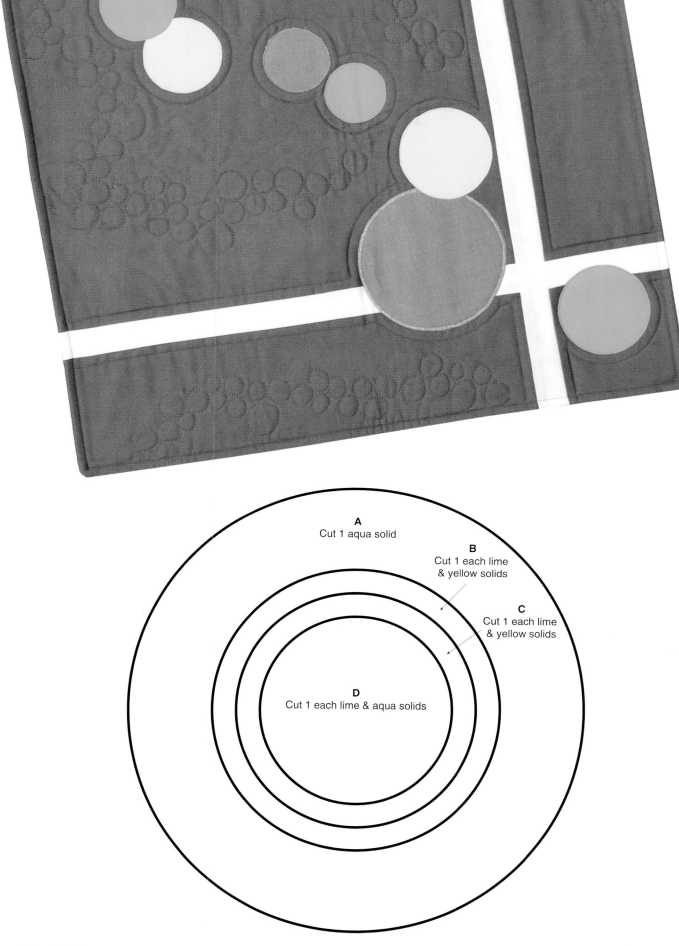

A
Cut 1 aqua solid

B
Cut 1 each lime
& yellow solids

C
Cut 1 each lime
& yellow solids

D
Cut 1 each lime & aqua solids

Saltwater Taffy

Design by Carolyn S. Vagts for the Village Pattern Company

Pick a palette of solid colors and create a fun and easy quilt that is perfect for a toddler or as a lap quilt. It all depends on the colors you choose.

Project Specifications

Skill Level: Confident Beginner
Quilt Size: 44" x 64"
Block Size: 4" x 4"
Number of Blocks: 30

Four-Patch
4" x 4" Block
Make 30

Materials

• Assorted solid scraps totaling 1⅛ yards
• 2¼ yards white solid (42½" usable width)
• Backing 52" x 72"
• Batting 52" x 72"
• All-purpose thread to match fabrics
• Quilting thread
• Basic sewing tools and supplies

Cutting

1. Cut 120 (2½") A squares from assorted solid scraps.

2. Cut 2¼" strips from the remaining assorted solid scraps to make a 228"-long strip after joining for binding.

3. Cut two 4½" by fabric width strips white solid; subcut strips into 30 (2½" x 4½") B rectangles.

4. Cut 10 (4½" x 42½") C strips white solid.

5. Cut 2 (2½" x 40½") D strips white solid.

6. Cut four 2½" by fabric width E strips white solid.

Completing the Blocks

1. Select four different-color A squares. Join two to make an A unit as shown in Figure 1; Press seam to one side. Repeat to make a total of 60 A units.

Figure 1

2. Select two A units and join with seams in opposite directions to complete one Four-Patch block referring to Figure 2; press seam to one side.

Make 30

Figure 2

3. Repeat step 2 to complete a total of 30 Four-Patch blocks.

Completing the Quilt Top

1. Select and join three Four-Patch blocks with three B rectangles and one C strip to make a pieced strip referring to Figure 3; press seams toward the B rectangles and the C strip. Repeat to make a total of 10 pieced strips.

Make 10

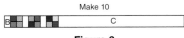

Figure 3

2. Join the pieced strips, turning every other strip as shown in the Placement Diagram, to complete the pieced center; press seams in one direction.

3. Sew the D strips to the top and bottom of the pieced center; press seams toward D strips.

4. Join the E strips on short ends to make one long strip; press seams open. Subcut strip into two 2½" x 64½" E strips.

5. Sew an E strip to opposite long sides of the pieced center to complete the quilt top.

Completing the Quilt

1. Sandwich the batting between the pieced quilt top and the prepared backing piece; pin or baste layers together to hold. Quilt as desired by hand or machine.

2. When quilting is complete, trim batting and backing fabric even with raw edges of the quilt top.

3. Join previously cut binding strips on short ends to make a 228"-long strip; press seams open.

4. Fold the binding strip with wrong sides together along length; press.

5. Sew binding to the quilt edges, mitering corners and overlapping ends. Fold binding to the back side and stitch in place to finish the quilt. ■

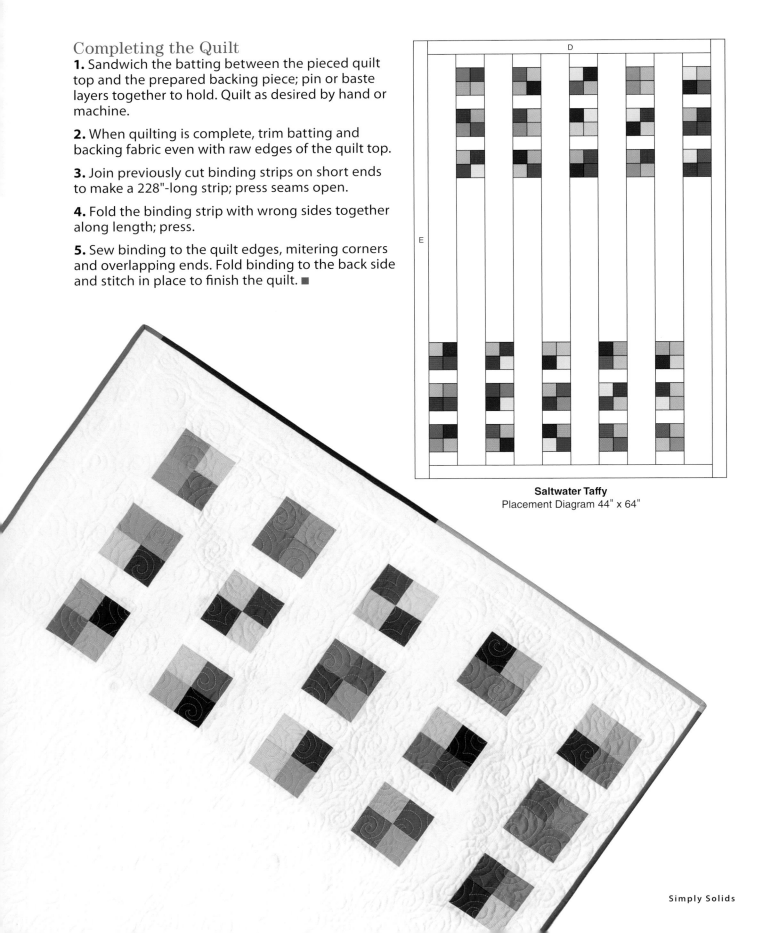

Saltwater Taffy
Placement Diagram 44" x 64"

Got a Penny?

Design by Connie Kauffman

If you like the look of wool penny rugs you will love this design. Create this bed runner from precut 5" squares.

Project Specifications
Skill Level: Confident Beginner
Bed Runner Size: 67½" x 22½" without prairie points
Block Size: 4½" x 4½"
Number of Blocks: 37

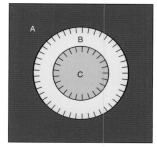

Penny
4½" x 4½" Block
Make 37

Materials
- 115 dark solid 5" A squares
- 56 light/medium solid 5" B/C squares
- Backing 68" x 23"
- Batting 68" x 23"
- Neutral-color all-purpose thread
- Black heavy-weight and all-purpose thread
- Quilting thread
- Template material
- 7 (8½" x 11") sheets lightweight fusible web
- Basic sewing tools and supplies

Cutting
1. Prepare templates for B and C pieces using patterns given. Trace 37 each B and C circles onto the paper side of the fusible web, leaving ¼" between circles. Cut out shapes, leaving a ⅛" margin around each one.

2. Select 37 B/C squares. Fuse a B circle to the wrong side of each of these squares. Cut out circles on traced lines and remove paper backings.

3. Fuse two C circles to the wrong side of each of the remaining B/C squares. Cut out circles on traced lines and remove paper backings. *Note: You will have an extra C circle, which can be used for another project.*

Completing the Penny Blocks
1. To complete one Penny block, select one each B and C circle of different colors and one dark solid A square.

2. Center and fuse the C circle onto the B circle.

3. Center and fuse the B-C circle to the A square.

4. Using the black heavy-weight thread in the top of the machine and black all-purpose thread in the bobbin, with a machine buttonhole stitch, stitch around the B and C circles to complete one Penny block referring to Figure 1.

Figure 1

5. Repeat steps 1–4 to complete a total of 37 Penny blocks.

Tip
The bed runner shown was quilted with X's in the A squares. With the appliquéd circles in the Penny blocks as the O's, this bed runner is filled with hugs and kisses.

Completing the Bed Runner

1. Arrange the Penny blocks with 38 A squares in a pleasing arrangement in five rows of 15 squares each, alternating the placement of the blocks in the rows referring to the Placement Diagram.

2. Join the squares and blocks as arranged to make five rows; press seams toward the A squares. Join the rows to complete the pieced top.

3. Fold the remaining 40 A squares in half on one diagonal and then in half on the diagonal again and press to make a prairie points as shown in Figure 2.

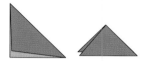

Figure 2

4. Arrange the prairie points around the outer edge, centering a prairie point on each square referring to Figure 3; baste in place to hold. *Note: Prairie points will overlap each other at ends.*

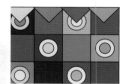

Figure 3

5. Place the batting on a flat surface with the backing right side up on top. Place the pieced top right sides together with the backing and pin layers together all around.

6. Stitch around edges of the pinned layers, leaving a 4" opening on one side for turning.

7. Clip corners and turn right side out through the opening. Press edges flat.

8. Turn opening edges to the inside ¼", press and hand-stitch the opening closed.

9. Quilt as desired to complete the bed runner. ■

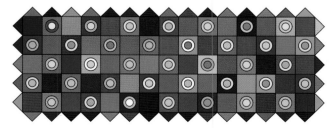

Got a Penny?
Placement Diagram 67½" x 22½"
without prairie points

Tip

The system of numbering thread weights is different from company to company. While some companies may use 12-weight thread for embellishment and Sashiko stitching, others don't manufacture a thread with that weight name. In general, you may use a heavier-weight thread, embroidery floss or pearl cotton to add buttonhole stitching by hand around each circle shape. If using a machine buttonhole stitch, use a heavier-weight thread in the top of the machine with all-purpose thread in the bobbin.

Practice stitching around circles on a sample before stitching on the circles in your project. Stitching a buttonhole stitch on a curve by machine requires practice to make stitching perfect.

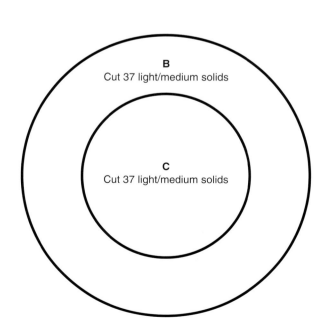

B
Cut 37 light/medium solids

C
Cut 37 light/medium solids

Beginner's Dream

Designed and Pieced by Jen Eskridge
Quilted by Evelyn Gernaat

Create a modern feel with solid fabrics and basic straight seam piecing. Change the colors to meet your needs.

Project Specifications
Skill Level: Beginner
Quilt Size: 72" x 96"
Block Size: 24" x 24"
Number of Blocks: 12

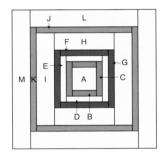

Beginner's Dream
24" x 24" Block
Make 12

Materials
- ½ yard pink solid
- ⅔ yard red solid
- 1⅛ yards orange solid
- 5½ yards cream solid
- Backing 80" x 104"
- Batting 80" x 104"
- Neutral-color all-purpose thread
- Quilting thread
- Basic sewing tools and supplies

Cutting
1. Cut one 4½" by fabric width strip pink solid; subcut strip into 24 (1½" x 4½") B strips.

2. Cut one 6½" by fabric width strip pink solid; subcut strip into 24 (1½" x 6½") C strips.

3. Cut one 8½" by fabric width strip red solid; subcut strip into 24 (1½" x 8½") F strips.

4. Cut one 10½" by fabric width strip red solid; subcut strip into 24 (1½" x 10½") G strips.

5. Cut one 16½" by fabric width strip orange solid; subcut strip into 24 (1½" x 16½") J strips.

6. Cut one 18½" by fabric width strip orange solid; subcut strip into 24 (1½" x 18½") K strips.

7. Cut two 4½" by fabric width strips cream solid; subcut strips into 12 (4½") A squares.

8. Cut one 6½" by fabric width strip cream solid; subcut strip into 24 (1½" x 6½") D strips.

9. Cut one 8½" by fabric width strip cream solid; subcut strip into 24 (1½" x 8½") E strips.

10. Cut two 10½" by fabric width strips cream solid; subcut strips into 24 (3½" x 10½") H strips.

11. Cut two 16½" by fabric width strips cream solid; subcut strips into 24 (3½" x 16½") I strips.

12. Cut two 18½" by fabric width strips cream solid; subcut strips 24 (3½" x 18½") L strips.

13. Cut two 24½" by fabric width strips cream solid; subcut strips into 24 (3½" x 24½") M strips.

14. Cut nine 2¼" by fabric width strips cream solid for binding.

Completing the Blocks
1. Starting in the center with an A square, sew B to opposite sides and then C to the remaining sides as shown in Figure 1; press seams toward B and C strips.

Figure 1

2. Continue to add strips to the pieced center in alphabetical order in the same manner as in step 1 to complete one Beginner's Dream block referring to Figure 2; press seams toward the most recently added strips before adding the next lettered strips.

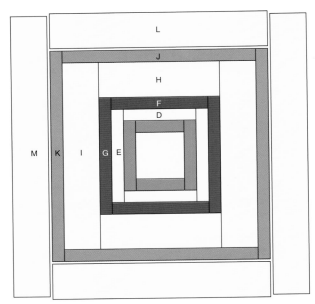

Figure 2

3. Repeat steps 1 and 2 to complete a total of 12 blocks.

Completing the Quilt Top

1. Arrange and join three Beginner's Dream blocks to make a row, orienting all the blocks in the row in the same position referring to the Placement Diagram; press seams in one direction. Repeat to make a total of four rows.

2. Join the rows, alternating the seam pressing direction in the rows, to complete the pieced top; press seams in one direction.

Completing the Quilt

1. Sandwich the batting between the pieced quilt top and the prepared backing piece; pin or baste layers together to hold. Quilt as desired by hand or machine.

2. When quilting is complete, trim batting and backing fabric even with raw edges of the quilt top.

3. Join previously cut binding strips on short ends with diagonal seams to make one long strip as shown in Figure 3; trim seams to ¼" and press seams open.

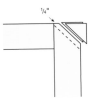

Figure 3

4. Fold the binding strip with wrong sides together along length; press.

5. Sew binding to the quilt edges, mitering corners and overlapping ends. Fold binding to the back side and stitch in place to finish the quilt. ■

Beginner's Dream
Placement Diagram 72" x 96"

Every Which Way

Design by Leanna Spanner

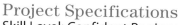

Create a fun and visually interesting quilt with the use of solids and strip piecing.

Project Specifications
Skill Level: Confident Beginner
Quilt Size: 60" x 84"
Block Size: 12" x 12"
Number of Blocks: 35

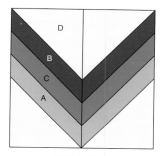

Which Way
12" x 12" Block
Make 35

Materials
- 1¼ yards lime green solid
- 1¼ yards blue solid
- 1⅞ yards teal solid
- 2⅔ yards cream solid
- Batting 68" x 92"
- Backing 68" x 92"
- Neutral-color all-purpose thread
- Quilting thread
- Basic sewing tools and supplies

Cutting
1. Cut 18 (1⅞" by fabric width) strips each lime green (A), blue (B) and teal (C) solids. Cut each strip in half to make 36 (1⅞" x 21") strips each fabric.

2. Cut eight 2¼" by fabric width strips teal solid for binding.

3. Cut 12 (6⅞" by fabric width) strips cream solid. Subcut strips into 70 (6⅞") squares. Cut each square in half on one diagonal to make 140 D triangles.

Completing the Blocks
1. Sew an A strip to a C strip to a B strip, staggering the strips 2" at the ends to make an A-B-C strip set as shown in Figure 1. Repeat to make 18 A-B-C strip sets.

Figure 1

2. Trim the A-B-C strip sets at the right staggered end (or at a 45-degree angle) referring to Figure 2.

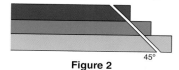

Figure 2

3. Cut each strip into two 9¼" A-B-C units to total 35 units referring to Figure 3.

Figure 3

4. Repeat steps 1–3, staggering strips in the opposite direction to cut 35 reversed 9¼" A-B-C units as shown in Figure 4.

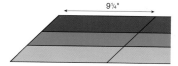

Figure 4

5. To complete one Which Way block, select one each A-B-C and reversed A-B-C unit and four D triangles.

6. Sew a D triangle to each side of each of the pieced units as shown in Figure 5; press seams toward D.

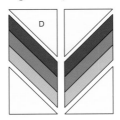

Figure 5

7. Join the pieced units referring to Figure 6 to complete one Which Way block; press seam to one side.

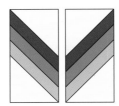

Figure 6

8. Repeat steps 5–7 to complete a total of 35 Which Way blocks.

Every Which Way
Placement Diagram 60" x 84"

Completing the Quilt

1. Select and join five Which Way blocks to make a row as shown in Figure 7. Press seams in one direction.

Figure 7

2. Repeat step 1 to make a total of seven rows, pressing seams in three rows in one direction and in four rows in the opposite direction.

3. Join the rows to complete the quilt top, alternating the pressing direction of the rows when joining. Press seams in one direction.

Completing the Quilt

1. Sandwich the batting between the pieced quilt top and the prepared backing piece; pin or baste layers together to hold. Quilt as desired by hand or machine.

2. When quilting is complete, trim batting and backing fabric even with raw edges of the quilt top.

3. Join previously cut binding strips on short ends with diagonal seams to make one long strip as shown in Figure 8; trim seams to ¼" and press seams open.

Figure 8

4. Fold the binding strip with wrong sides together along length; press.

5. Sew binding to the quilt edges, mitering corners and overlapping ends. Fold binding to the back side and stitch in place to finish the quilt. ■

Vintage Drunkard's Path

Design by Darlene Zimmerman

This quilt is a blast from the past. Solid fabrics make it a timeless classic whether you like vintage or contemporary.

Project Specifications

Skill Level: Intermediate
Quilt Size: 64½" x 88½"
Block Size: 12" x 12"
Number of Blocks: 35

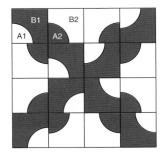

Drunkard's Path
12" x 12" Block
Make 35

Materials

- 4 yards white solid
- 5¼ yards red solid
- Backing 73" x 97"
- Batting 73" x 97"
- All-purpose thread to match fabrics
- Quilting thread
- Template material
- Basic sewing tools and supplies

Cutting

1. Prepare templates for A1/A2 and B1/B2 pieces using patterns given.

2. Cut 24 (3½" by fabric width) strips each red and white solids; subcut strips from each fabric into 280 (3½") squares.

3. Using template B1/B2, trim away the small curved corner from each square referring to Figure 1.

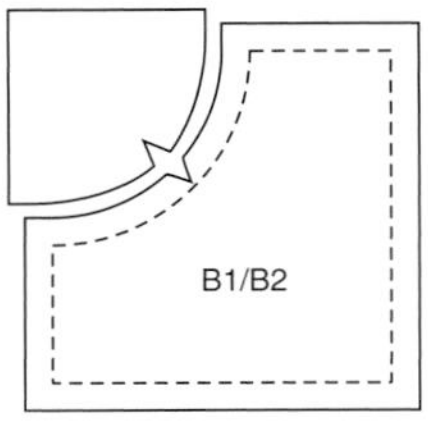

Figure 1

4. Cut 18 (2½" by fabric width) strips each red and white solids; subcut strips from each fabric into 280 (2½") squares.

5. Using the A1/A2 template, cut the curve to make A1/A2 pieces referring to Figure 2.

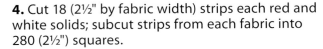

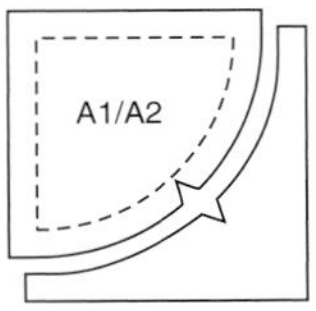

A1/A2

Figure 2

6. Cut eight 2¾" by fabric width C/D strips red solid.

7. Cut eight 2¼" by fabric width strips red solid for binding.

Completing the Blocks

1. Sew A1 to B1 to make an A1-B1 unit as shown in Figure 3.

Make 280

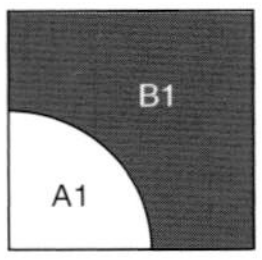

B1

A1

Figure 3

2. Clip curves and press seam toward B1 referring to Figure 4.

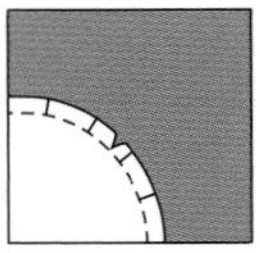

Figure 4

3. Repeat steps 1 and 2 to complete a total of 280 A1-B1 units.

4. Sew A2 to B2 to complete an A2-B2 unit as shown in Figure 5.

Make 280

B2

A2

Figure 5

5. Clip curves and press seam toward B2 referring to Figure 6.

Figure 6

6. Repeat steps 4 and 5 to complete a total of 280 A2-B2 units.

7. To complete one Drunkard's Path block, select and arrange eight each A1-B1 and A2-B2 units in four rows of four units each referring to Figure 7 for positioning of pieces. Join units in each row, pressing seams in adjoining rows in opposite directions.

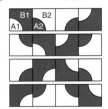

B1 B2
A1 A2

Figure 7

 8. Join the rows to complete one Drunkard's Path block; press seams in one direction.

9. Repeat steps 7 and 8 to complete a total of 35 Drunkard's Path blocks.

Completing the Quilt Top

1. Arrange and join five Drunkard's Path blocks to make a row, turning the blocks to alternate the seam-pressing direction. Press seams in one direction. Repeat to make a total of seven rows.

2. Join the rows, alternating the seam-pressing direction, to complete the pieced center; press seams in one direction.

3. Join the C/D strips on the short ends to make a long strip; press seams open. Subcut strip into two 84½" C strips and two 65" D strips.

4. Sew C strips to opposite long sides and D strips to the top and bottom of the pieced center to complete the quilt top; press seams toward C and D strips.

Completing the Quilt

1. Sandwich the batting between the pieced quilt top and the prepared backing piece; pin or baste layers together to hold. Quilt as desired by hand or machine.

2. When quilting is complete, trim batting and backing fabric even with raw edges of the quilt top.

3. Join previously cut binding strips on short ends with diagonal seams to make one long strip as shown in Figure 8; trim seams to ¼" and press seams open.

¼"

Figure 8

Vintage Drunkard's Path
Placement Diagram 64½" x 88½"

4. Fold the binding strip with wrong sides together along length; press.

5. Sew binding to the quilt edges, mitering corners and overlapping ends. Fold binding to the back side and stitch in place to finish the quilt. ■

Tip

When joining curved pieces such as those used in the Drunkard's Path units, match the center notches and pin, then match ends and pin. Ease in the area between the pins, matching the edges as you sew.

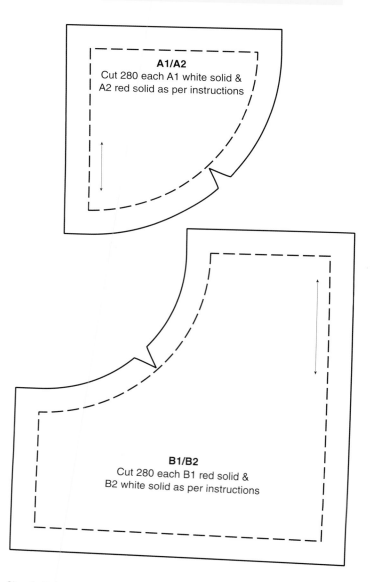

A1/A2
Cut 280 each A1 white solid &
A2 red solid as per instructions

B1/B2
Cut 280 each B1 red solid &
B2 white solid as per instructions

Bow Ties

Design by Nancy McNally

Are you up for a challenge? Perfect your technique for making "Y" seams while you create a stunning throw-size quilt.

Project Specifications
Skill Level: Advanced
Quilt Size: 55¾" x 58"
Block Size: 8" x 14"
Number of Blocks: 23

Mulberry Bow Tie
8" x 14" Block
Make 8

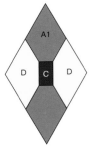

Green Bow Tie
8" x 14" Block
Make 15

Materials
- 1 yard brown solid
- 2¼ yards green solid
- 2⅜ yards mulberry solid
- 3¾ yards cream solid
- Backing 64" x 66"
- Batting 64" x 66"
- Neutral-color all-purpose thread
- Quilting thread
- Template material
- Basic sewing tools and supplies

Cutting
Prepare templates using pattern pieces given; ... directed on each piece, setting aside B, C, G ... pieces to cut from leftover brown solid from ... n steps 5 and 6.

... e 3½" by fabric width I strips green solid.

... ½" x 40¼" J strips green solid.

... y fabric width strips green solid

5. Cut one 3½" by fabric width strip brown solid; subcut into four 3½" R squares. Use remainder of strip to cut B, C, G and H pieces.

6. Cut one 5½" by fabric width strip brown solid; subcut into four 5½" Q squares. Use remainder of strip to cut B, C, G and H pieces.

Completing the Blocks
1. Transfer seam-allowance dots from templates to each pattern.

2. To make one Green Bow Tie block, select and join two A1 pieces with C at the short ends, stopping stitching at the marked dots as shown in Figure 1; press seams toward A1.

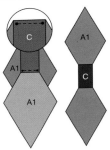

Figure 1

3. Sew a D piece to one side of the A1-C unit starting stitching at one marked seam-allowance dot on the D piece and stitching to the opposite marked end as shown in Figure 2.

Figure 2

4. Starting at the inside edge of D, sew D to one side of one A1 piece referring to Figure 3.

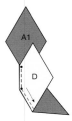

Figure 3

5. Repeat step 4 with the other inside edge of D and the second A1 piece to complete one side of the block referring to Figure 4.

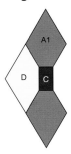

Figure 4

6. Repeat steps 3–5 with a second D piece on the opposite side of the pieced section to complete one Green Bow Tie block as shown in Figure 5.

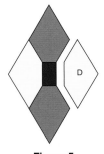

Figure 5

Tip

Use a small hole punch to cut holes at seam intersections on templates as marked on patterns with dots. Place the template on the wrong side of fabric piece and use a fabric-marking pen inserted in each punched hole to mark seam intersections.

7. Press seams toward D.

8. Repeat steps 2–7 to complete a total of 15 Green Bow Tie blocks.

9. Repeat steps 2–7 with A2 pieces to complete a total of eight Mulberry Bow Tie blocks referring to Figure 6.

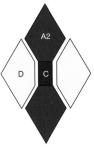

Figure 6

Completing the Pieced Units

1. Select one each A2, B, E and ER piece to make one top/bottom unit.

2. Sew B to A2 and set in E and ER with set-in or Y seams to complete one top/bottom unit as shown in Figure 7; press seams toward B and then E and ER.

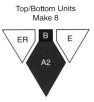

Figure 7

3. Repeat steps 1 and 2 to complete a total of eight top/bottom units.

4. To complete one side unit, select one each D, H, F and FR piece.

5. Join the F and FR piece with H and set in the D piece referring to Figure 8; press seams toward H and then D. Repeat to make a total of four side units.

Figure 8

6. Select one each F, G and E piece to make one corner unit.

7. Sew G to F and set in E to complete one corner unit referring to Figure 9; press seam toward G and then E. Repeat to make a second corner unit.

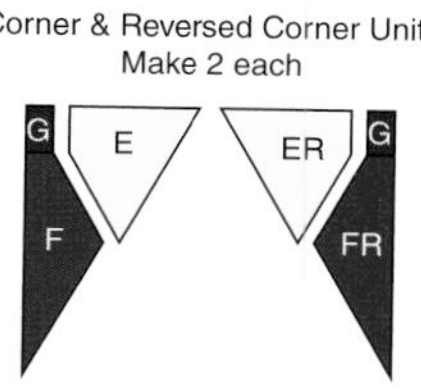

Corner & Reversed Corner Units
Make 2 each

Figure 9

8. Repeat step 7 with G, FR and ER pieces to make two reversed corner units, again referring to Figure 9.

Completing the Top
1. Arrange and join the pieced blocks with the top/bottom units, side units, corner and reversed corner units to make diagonal rows referring to Figure 10; press seams in adjacent rows in opposite directions.

Figure 10

2. Join the rows to complete the pieced center; press seams in one direction.

3. Join I strips on the short ends to make a long strip; press seams open. Subcut strip into two 3½" x 42½" I strips.

4. Sew I strips to opposite sides of the pieced center; press seams toward I strips.

5. Sew an R square to each end of each J strip; press seams toward J. Sew these strips to the top and bottom of the pieced center; press seams toward the R/J strips.

6. Sew M to opposite sides of K1 as shown in Figure 11; press seams toward M. Repeat to make a second K1-M unit.

Make 2

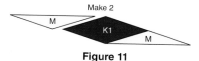

Figure 11

7. Sew M to K2 and add L and LR to make a side end unit as shown in Figure 12; repeat to make a second unit. Sew these units to one K1-M unit to complete one side strip as shown in Figure 13. Repeat to make a second side strip.

Side End Unit
Make 4

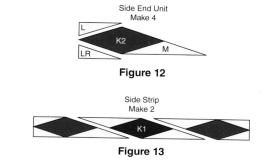

Figure 12

Side Strip
Make 2

Figure 13

8. Repeat steps 6 and 7 with the N1, N2, O, OR and P pieces to make a top and a bottom strip as shown in Figure 14.

Top and Bottom Strip
Make 2

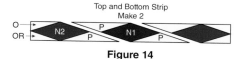

Figure 14

9. Sew a Q square to opposite ends of each top and bottom strip; press seams toward Q.

10. Sew a side strip to the I sides and the top and bottom strips to the J sides of the bordered center to complete the quilt top referring to the Placement Diagram; press seams toward the I and J strips.

Completing the Quilt
1. Sandwich the batting between the pieced quilt top and the prepared backing piece; pin or baste layers together to hold. Quilt as desired by hand or machine.

2. When quilting is complete, trim batting and backing fabric even with raw edges of the quilt top.

3. Join previously cut binding strips on short ends with diagonal seams to make one long strip as shown in Figure 15; trim seams to ¼" and press seams open.

Figure 15

4. Fold the binding strip with wrong sides together along length; press.

5. Sew binding to the quilt edges, mitering corners and overlapping ends. Fold binding to the back side and stitch in place to finish the quilt. ■

Bow Ties
Placement Diagram 55¾" x 58"

Tip

To make set-in or Y seams, it is important to mark the seam-allowance intersections and stop sewing at the marks to allow the fabric to turn after the seam has been stitched.

To make a Y seam, start stitching from the inside marked seam and stitch toward the outer edge of the seam. In most cases, the seam ends at the edge of the fabric as shown in Figure 16. However, in this project, the beginning and ending of the seams between the C and A pieces are marked dots at the seam allowances as shown in Figure 17.

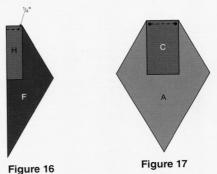

Figure 16   **Figure 17**

It is important to secure the stitching with reverse stitches at the end of Y seams because these seams are not included inside another seam, so they can easily come apart when stressed.

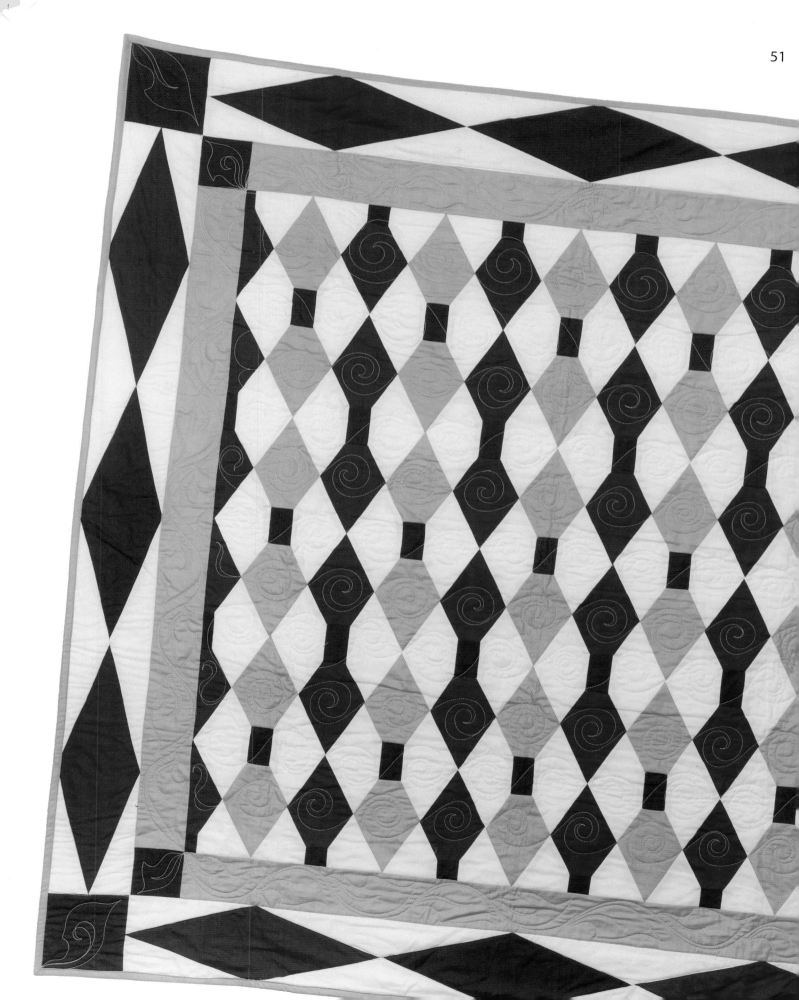

Bow Ties
Continued

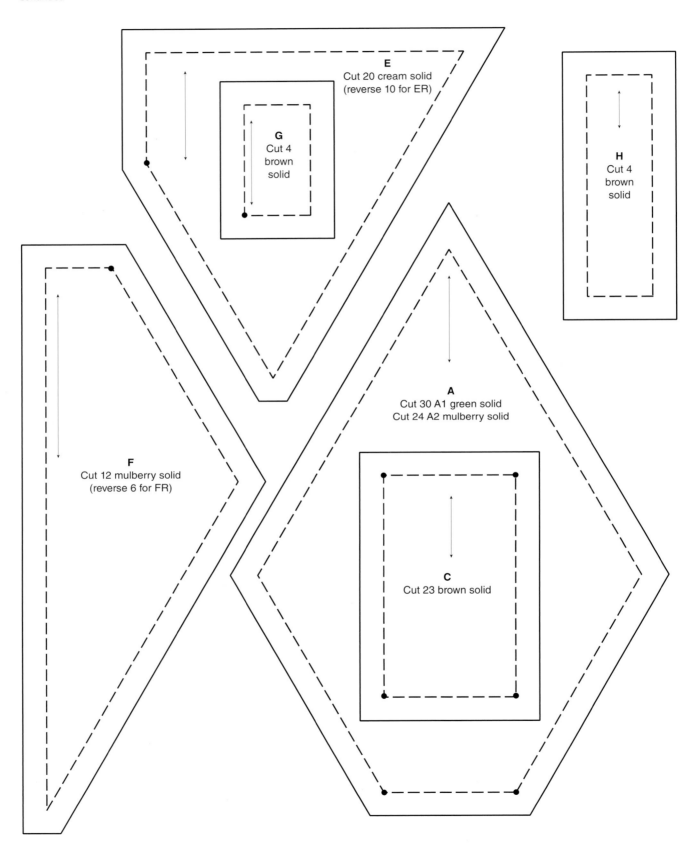

E
Cut 20 cream solid
(reverse 10 for ER)

G
Cut 4
brown
solid

H
Cut 4
brown
solid

F
Cut 12 mulberry solid
(reverse 6 for FR)

A
Cut 30 A1 green solid
Cut 24 A2 mulberry solid

C
Cut 23 brown solid

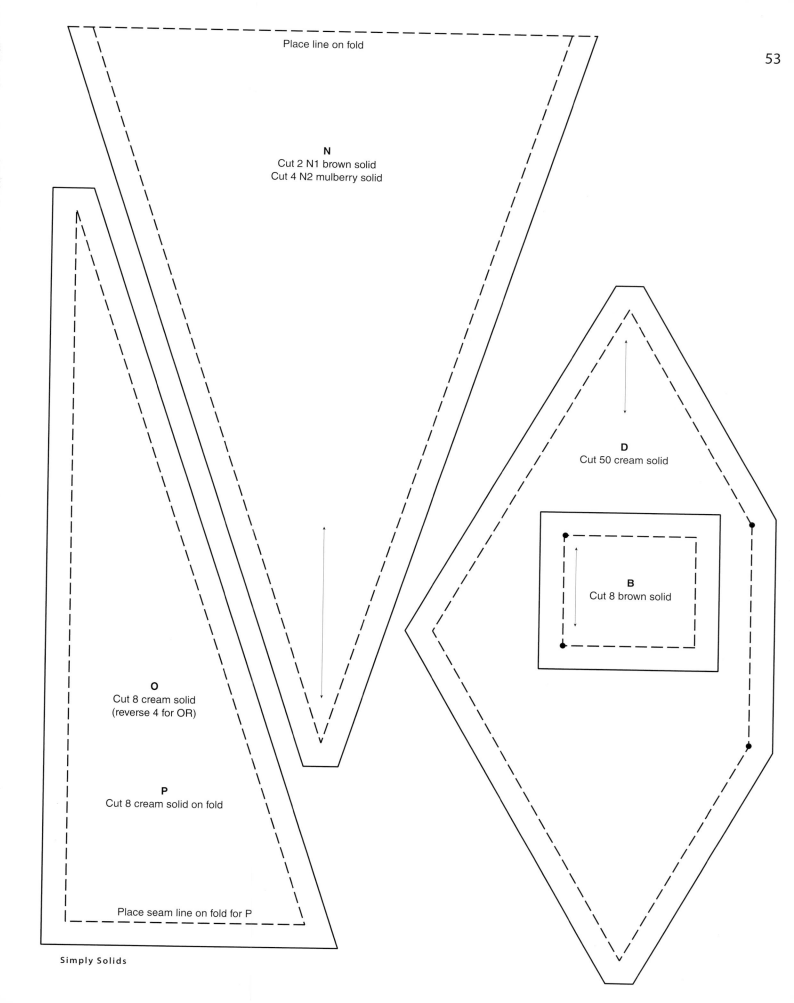

Place line on fold

N
Cut 2 N1 brown solid
Cut 4 N2 mulberry solid

D
Cut 50 cream solid

B
Cut 8 brown solid

O
Cut 8 cream solid
(reverse 4 for OR)

P
Cut 8 cream solid on fold

Place seam line on fold for P

Simply Solids

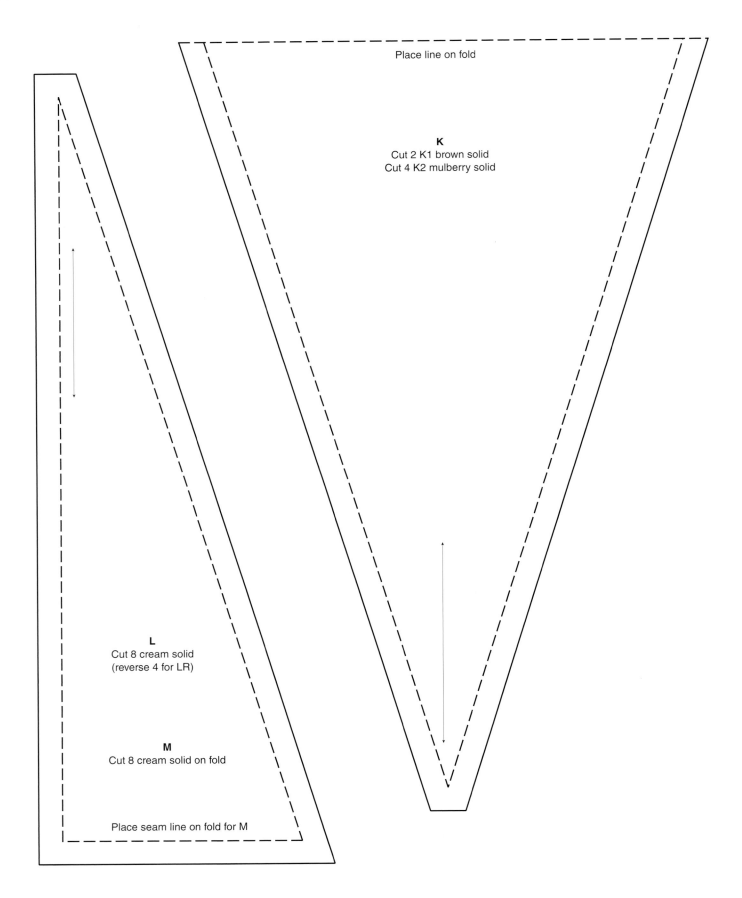

Place line on fold

K
Cut 2 K1 brown solid
Cut 4 K2 mulberry solid

L
Cut 8 cream solid
(reverse 4 for LR)

M
Cut 8 cream solid on fold

Place seam line on fold for M

Special Thanks

Designers used the latest fabrics and supplies in many of the projects in *Simply Solids*. In some cases, another quilter helped finish the project.

We would like to thank these individuals and/or manufacturers for their generosity.

Card Trick Again, page 16: Kona® Cotton Solids and Nature's Flora fabric collections from Robert Kaufman; Nature-Fil™ batting from Fairfield; Star Machine Quilting thread from Coats.

Modern Country, page 20: Cotton Supreme Solids from RJR Fabrics; Tuscany Silk batting from Hobbs; Mako 50 cotton thread from Aurifil.

Tiny Bubbles, page 26: Bella Solids fabrics from Moda.

Saltwater Taffy, page 30: Saltwater Taffy and Cotton Couture fabric collections from Michael Miller Fabrics.

Got a Penny?, page 33: Charm Square Packs in Cotton Solids Dark Palette (3 packs) and Dusty Palette (2 packs), and black Kona® Cotton from Robert Kaufman; Soft and Bright batting and Light Steam-A-Seam2 from The Warm Company; Black (12 wt. and 30 wt.) thread from Sulky®.

Bow Ties, page 46: Bella Solids from Moda.

Annie's™ *Simply Solids* is published by Annie's, 306 East Parr Road, Berne, IN 46711. Printed in USA. Copyright © 2012, 2013 Annie's. All rights reserved. This publication may not be reproduced in part or in whole without written permission from the publisher.

RETAIL STORES: If you would like to carry this pattern book or any other Annie's publications, visit AnniesWSL.com.

Every effort has been made to ensure that the instructions in this pattern book are complete and accurate. We cannot, however, take responsibility for human error, typographical mistakes or variations in individual work. Please visit AnniesCustomerCare.com to check for pattern updates.

ISBN: 978-1-59217-468-3

2 3 4 5 6 7 8 9

Photo Index

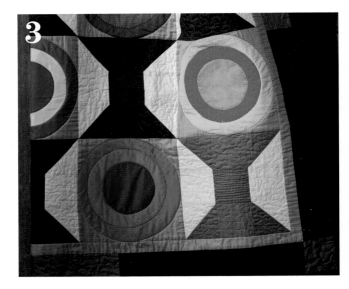

3

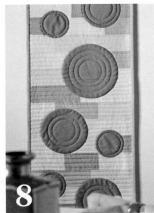

8

12

16

20

26

30

33

36

39

42

46